Swinging at a school playground in Tanzania

Come Out and Play

A Global Journey

Maya Ajmera • John D. Ivanko

Running in the snow in the United States

Charlesbridge

To play means swinging, jumping,

Jumping rope in Burkina Faso

Hopping through a sprinkler in Austria

Playing leapfrog in Laos

Splashing through puddles in India

running, and climbing.

Circling a pole in Bolivia

Searching for butterflies in South Africa

Scaling a climbing wall in France

To play means bouncing, tossing,

Throwing a Frisbee in Japan

Bouncing a ball in Tanzania

Playing cricket in Sri Lanka

hitting, and kicking.

Playing ice hockey in Serbia

Kicking a soccer ball in Brazil

Swinging at a softball in the United States

Hitting a tennis ball in China

To play means flying kites, chasing bubbles,

Running with kites in a field in Bangladesh

Putting a kite in the air in Madagascar

Popping bubbles in Mexico

Cooling off with a buddy in a river in Thailand

splashing in water,
and riding on bikes
and skateboards.

Pedaling a bicycle in Romania

Balancing on a skateboard in Canada

To play means making things . . .

Painting a craft-stick sculpture in the United Kingdom

Building a wire truck in Kenya

Making toy cars out of cans in Madagascar

and using your imagination.

Dreaming of flying in South Korea

Imagining a space adventure in the United States

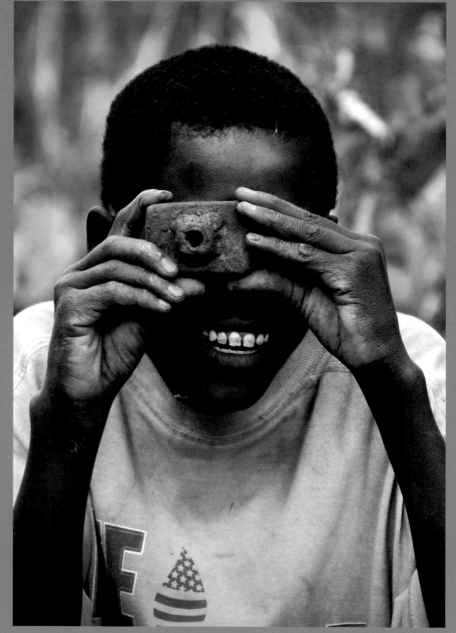

Pretending to be a photographer in Ethiopia

Hanging from a giant steering wheel in New Zealand

You can play all kinds of games . . .

Making a chess move in Spain

Playing jacks in Guatemala

Playing table tennis in the Czech Republic

in all kinds of places.

Counting mancala markers in Uganda

Climbing on hay bales in Estonia

Dancing in old church ruins in the Philippines

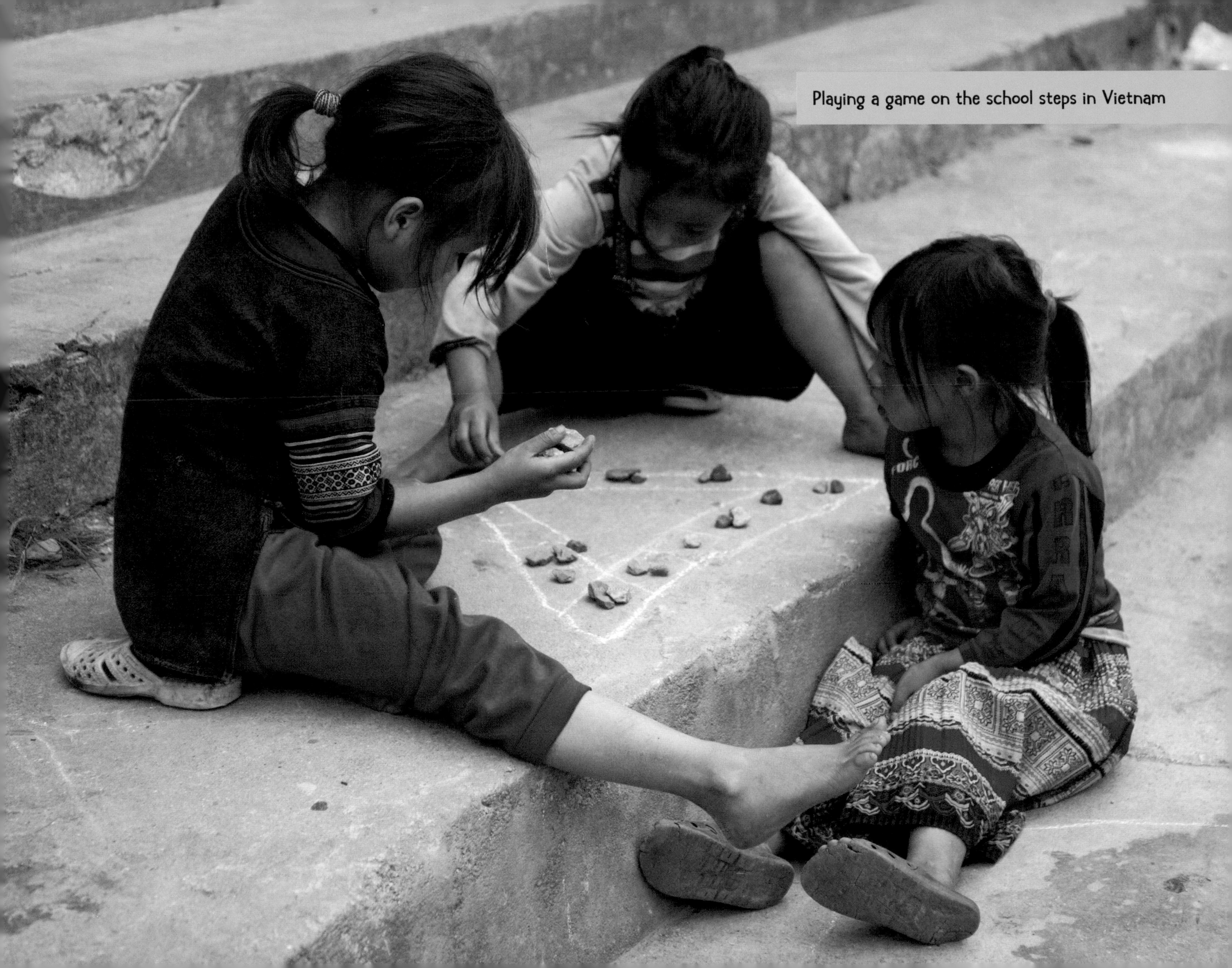

Playing a game on the school steps in Vietnam

Putting together a puzzle in the United Kingdom

You can play quietly or shout with laughter.

Typing on a tablet computer in Australia

Hanging out in a hammock in Sweden

Goofing around at a lake in Malawi

Playing music on a handmade instrument in Ethiopia

Whether you play on your own or with your friends and family,

Shaking paws with a dog in Burma

Going for a piggyback ride in Mongolia

Playing basketball together in the United States

to play means having fun!

Crawling through a tire at a playground in Iran

Splashing at a water park in the United States

Holding on tight to a rope swing in Nepal

Laughing in the rain in Mali

All Kinds of Toys

Almost anything can be a toy. A toy can be a truck you make from wire or a house you build from a cardboard box. Toys such as jump ropes, hoops, stilts, kites, and balls are found all over the world. What is your favorite toy?

Places to Play

You can play anywhere and everywhere. Swinging, jumping, running, and climbing often need wide-open spaces. Other types of play are best done inside, especially when the weather is rainy or cold. Parks and playgrounds are special places to have fun. But sometimes your own backyard can be the best place of all. Where is your favorite place to play?

Lots of Games

There are many kinds of games. Checkers, chess, and go fish are games in which you try to be more clever than the other players. Table tennis, hide-and-seek, and tag are games in which speed and coordination are very important. Cooperation and teamwork are a big part of games such as baseball and hockey. You can create whole new worlds with computer games like Minecraft. What is your favorite game?

Playing Minecraft on a computer in Germany

Kids everywhere love to play.

Estonia
Ukraine
Turkey
Iran
Saudi Arabia
Ethiopia
Uganda
Kenya
Tanzania
Malawi
Madagascar
Mongolia
South Korea
Japan
China
Nepal
Burma
Laos
India
Bangladesh
Vietnam
Thailand
Cambodia
Philippines
Sri Lanka
Australia
New Zealand

Using Your Imagination

There are no limits when you use your imagination. It lets you travel to distant lands, make new friends, build wonderful things, and enjoy exciting adventures. When you pretend to be a pilot, an astronaut, or a mother or father, you are creating a world that is all your own. How do you like to make believe?

Playing a card game with friends in China

Friends

Play brings friends together. Whether you are hanging out, competing against each other, or just goofing off, friends help make play fun. Joking around and making silly faces bring lots of laughter. Sharing toys, joining in games, and spending time together can help a friendship grow into something that lasts a lifetime. Can you come out and play?

To my daughter, Talia, who loves to play, explore, and have fun by herself and with her friends. Children everywhere have the right to play.—M. A.

To my son, Liam Kivirist, and to children everywhere. May they never lose that sense of joy, discovery, and creativity that comes with play.—J. D. I.

Maya Ajmera would like to extend her deepest thanks to Adele Richardson Ray for her support of *Come Out and Play*.

Text copyright © 2020 by Maya Ajmera and John D. Ivanko
Photographs copyright © by individual copyright holders
All rights reserved, including the right of reproduction in whole or in part in any form.
Charlesbridge and colophon are registered trademarks of Charlesbridge Publishing, Inc.

At the time of publication, any URLs printed in this book were accurate and active. Charlesbridge and the authors are not responsible for the content or accessibility of any website.

Published by Charlesbridge
85 Main Street, Watertown, MA 02472
(617) 926-0329 · www.charlesbridge.com

Library of Congress Cataloging-in-Publication Data
Names: Ajmera, Maya author.
Title: Come out and play: a global journey / Maya Ajmera and John D. Ivanko.
Description: Watertown, Massachusetts : Charlesbridge, in support of the Global Fund for Children, [2020]
Identifiers: LCCN 2019014544 (print) | LCCN 2019021834 (ebook) |
ISBN 9781623541637 (reinforced for library use) | ISBN 9781632899590 (ebook) |
ISBN 9781632899606 (ebook pdf)
Subjects: LCSH: Play—Juvenile literature. | Outdoor recreation—Juvenile literature. |
Outdoor games—Juvenile literature. | Games—Juvenile literature. | Handicraft—
Juvenile literature. | Toy making—Juvenile literature. | Creative activities and seat
work—Juvenile literature. | Amusements—Juvenile literature. | Play environments—
Juvenile literature.
Classification: LCC GV182.9 (ebook) | LCC GV182.9 .A56 2020 (print) |
DDC 649/.5—dc23
LC record available at https://lccn.loc.gov/2019014544

Printed in Singapore
(hc) 10 9 8 7 6 5 4 3 2 1

Display type set in Canvas Text Sans by Yellow Design Studio
Text type set in Digby by Atlantic Fonts
Color separations by Colourscan Print Co Pte Ltd in Singapore
Manufactured by C.O.S. Printers Pte Ltd in Singapore
Production supervision by Brian G. Walker
Designed by Jacqueline Noelle Cote

Running along a beach in the United States

Photo Credits: FRONT COVER: © Juice Images/age fotostock. BACK COVER: StockPlanets/iStock. TITLE PAGE: p. 1: © BLM Photo/Alamy Stock Photo. SWINGING, JUMPING: p. 2: © Joerg Boethling/Alamy Stock Photo. p. 3: left, © Photononstop/Alamy Stock Photo; top right, © amriphoto/iStock; bottom right, © Buntoon Rodseng/Shutterstock.com. RUNNING, CLIMBING: p. 4: © Tim Gainey/Alamy Stock Photo. p. 5: top left, © Jacques Jangoux/Alamy Stock Photo; bottom left, © Gregg Vignal/Alamy Stock Photo; right, © BSIP SA/Alamy Stock Photo. BOUNCING, TOSSING: p. 6: left, © Gillian Lloyd/Alamy Stock Photo; top right, © Hakase_/iStock; bottom right, © Zoonar/I Tykhyi/age fotostock. p. 7: © Tim Gainey/Alamy Stock Photo. HITTING, KICKING: p. 8: left, © Lucky Business/Shutterstock.com; top right, © Aflo Co., Ltd./Alamy Stock Photo; bottom right, © Susan Leggett/Alamy Stock Photo. p. 9: © Leung Cho Pan/Panther Media/age fotostock. FLYING KITES, CHASING BUBBLES: p. 10: left, © M Yousuf Tushar/Majority World/age fotostock; right, © Asael Anthony/hemis/age fotostock. p. 11: © aldomurillo/iStock. SPLASHING, RIDING BIKES AND SKATEBOARDS: p. 12: © Sirisak_baokaew/Shutterstock.com. p. 13: left, © Daniel Chetroni/Shutterstock.com; right, © Hero Images, Inc./Alamy Stock Photo. MAKING THINGS: p. 14: left, © Andrew Fox/Alamy Stock Photo; right, © Friedrich Stark/Alamy Stock Photo. p. 15: © Danita Delimont/Alamy Stock Photo. USING IMAGINATION: p. 16: top left, © Topic Photo Agency/age fotostock; bottom left, © RyanJLane/iStock; right, © Pascal Mannaerts/Alamy Stock Photo. p. 17: © doble-d/iStock. INSIDE, OUTSIDE: p. 18: © Tim Cuff/Alamy Stock Photo. p. 19: left, © Krysja/Shutterstock.com; top right, © ridvan_celik/iStock; bottom right, © imageBROKER/Alamy Stock Photo. ALL KINDS OF GAMES: p. 20: © Michele Burgess/Alamy Stock Photo. p. 21: left, © Danita Delimont/Al12amy Stock Photo; top right, © Ramon Espelt/Westend61/age fotostock; bottom right, © Daniel Vrabec/Alamy Stock Photo. ALL KINDS OF PLACES: p. 22: top left, © Jake Lyell/Alamy Stock Photo; bottom left, © Jaak Nilson/age fotostock; right, © Art Phaneuf/Alamy Stock Photo. p. 23: © MindStorm/Shutterstock.com. PLAY QUIETLY OR SHOUT WITH LAUGHTER: p. 24: © Andrew Fox/Alamy Stock Photo. p. 25: top left, © redbrickstock.com/Alamy Stock Photo; bottom left, © David Schreiner/Folio Images/Alamy Stock Photo; right, © Graham Prentice/Alamy Stock Photo. ON YOUR OWN OR WITH FRIENDS AND FAMILY: p. 26: © Lost Horizon Images/Cultura/age fotostock. p. 27: left, © isarescheewin/Shutterstock.com; top right, © Paul Brown/Alamy Stock Photo; bottom right, © Monkey Business Images/Shutterstock.com. HAVING FUN: p. 28: top left, © Shehzad Noorani/Majority World/age fotostock; bottom left: © ZUMA Press, Inc./Alamy Stock Photo; right: © Friedrich Stark/Alamy Stock Photo. p. 29: © Riccardo Lennart Niels Mayer/Alamy Stock Photo. KIDS EVERYWHERE LOVE TO PLAY: p. 30: © Georg Wendt/dpa/age fotostock. p. 31: © David Keith Brown/Alamy Stock Photo. COPYRIGHT PAGE: p. 32: © John D. Ivanko.

Photo Research: Julie Alissi/J8 Media